Writing Exercises For The Reluctant Writer

Writing Exercises For The Reluctant Writer

Gerald E. Forrest

Pentland Press, Inc.
England • USA • Scotland

PUBLISHED BY PENTLAND PRESS, INC.
5122 Bur Oak Circle, Raleigh, North Carolina 27612
United States of America
919-782-0281

ISBN 1-57197-203-X
Library of Congress Catalog Card Number 99-75264

Printed in the United States of America

Table of Contents

Foreword

Finally, someone has done it. Congratulations, Jerry, you've turned learning to write from pedantry to pleasure!

As a former teacher of English, I have labored (or my students have labored) through spelling, grammar, and syntax fearful that good writing was not possible without these fundamental tools. How many students did I turn off by insisting that tools come first, then writing?

During the '60s when I was the director of Innovations for the Palm Springs Unified School District, we experimented with several creative techniques for helping kids learn, such as: programmed instruction, learning labs, team teaching, and flexible scheduling. Teaching and writing on innovative ways escaped us, but it hasn't escaped Jerry.

Having been the instructor for many college and university training courses, I was constantly on the lookout for practical and palatable materials like Jerry's, but I didn't find them. Writers and/or professors couldn't seem to lift themselves out of the mire of traditional approaches into the reality of Jerry's down-to-earth approach.

I've been a teacher, counselor, dean of students, principal, director of instruction, consultant to medical centers and the Peace Corps and a member of Visiting Nurses Association. I sincerely wish that I had had Jerry's creative talents to supplement my efforts.

I've taken courses at Cal Tech, Occidental, UC and Harvard; I've never seen such interesting and useful materials as Jerry has created.

Jerry is on the cutting edge of innovative educational approaches in his book on "The Reluctant Writer."

Webster D. Wilson, Ed.D.
September 1999

Preface

The ability to write clearly is one way to fulfill the basic need to communicate. The sample exercises that follow have proven helpful in working with reluctant writers, especially those of junior high and high school age.

Many sources have provided input for the formulation of these exercises: books, magazines, newspapers, discarded library and grammar books, etc. While the materials appear quite ordinary, the approach has yielded extraordinary results.

Designed to jump start the young writer, these exercises do not pretend to address syntax, grammar, or spelling, except incidentally. Not geared to produce polished prose, the exercises serve as a vehicle to get these candidates writing . . . and enjoying it.

Every effort has been made to insure that the student writings are authentic. The author has validated by name each contribution and therefore assumes no responsibility for any oversights.

Acknowledgements

My sincere thanks to Dr. Joy Smith for her organizational skills in placing a large body of material into a recognizable form, chapter by chapter.

Many thanks also to Jewell Barger and her assistants for helping an old-fashioned teacher learn some of the mysteries of the word processor.

And to Brother Virgil Eastman, F.S.C., former English professor at St. Mary's College, thank you for urging your students to always strive for clarity.

Thanks to Counselor Patrick O'Brien, who was never too far away to offer expert advice and shepherd along this book—and me.

Finally, a huge "thank you" to the hundreds of former students who so generously offered their writings to be a part of this book. To them I dedicate all the efforts that have gone into its production.

Introduction

Here is a concise book of twelve easy lessons that will guide students, teachers, parents, professionals and those wishing to make a quantum leap in their ability to write with clarity and grace.

This easy to follow, step-by-step approach incorporates creativity and organization that will make writing letters, themes, essays, term papers, and, indeed, all writing more exciting and satisfying.

Each of the twelve units builds on the one before, yet is complete in itself. Each unit includes a description of the topic being taught and examples to use as models as well as suggestions for writing lab, spelling, and grammar exercises. Teachers, especially, will feel comfortable with these units, knowing they are teaching a short course in writing that will prove to be invaluable for their students.

Writing Exercises For The Reluctant Writer targets students, teachers, parents, professionals and others by serving as a handbook for improved writing. It also serves as a fingertip guide to ideas and fresh approaches. The student writings demonstrate the impact of these ideas and approaches while serving to inspire others to take a more satisfying path with their own writing strategies.

1

Sterile Sentences

Sterile sentences are flat and essentially lifeless. Most beginning writers use them ad nauseum, creating disinterest and boredom. Sterile sentences are deadly because they use a consistent, repetitious pattern: the subject, the predicate, and the object.

Example: *John hit the dog.*

A variety of measures may be used to break the pattern. The most effective measure is to use details as shown in the examples that follow.

Sentences are much more appealing when they are "dressed-up" with selective details such as action and color.

Another way to break the monotony of subject, predicate, and object is to answer the questions *who?*, *what?*, *where?*, *when?*, *why?*, *how?*, and *how much?* This is commonly referred to as "the journalistic approach to writing."

Daily Lesson Plan

1. *Writing Lab (8–10 minutes)*

The Writing Lab consists of giving the students *three* separate topics from the list in Chapter 13. These topics and questions have proven to be sure-fire writing starters. The students should write for about eight to ten minutes to complete the three paragraphs.

Hint: Tell the students to place a check next to the paragraph they consider to be their best writing. Ask the students to use examples whenever possible.

2. *Spelling (5 minutes)*

On the back of the Writing Lab paper, quiz the students on ten words from a list of "Most Commonly Misspelled Words." The students should correct their own papers and keep an account of their own spelling progress. Allow them approximately five minutes to complete the quiz.

3. *Grammar (12 minutes)*

The teacher may choose any good grammar workbook and have the students do one or two exercises on any topic that has proven to be a trouble spot for the class. The students should be allowed approximately twelve minutes to complete this exercise.

4. *Lesson for the Day (with Recommended Exercises, 30 minutes)*

To remedy sterile sentences, follow these guidelines:

A. Put details into sentences.

B. Use descriptive and active words.

C. Answer *who?, what?, when?, where?, why?,* and *how much?* in the sentences.

Below are some examples of sterile sentences and how they can be brought to life:

1. The boy hit the ball.

The skinny little freckled face boy took a major league swing and hit the ball into center field.

—?

2. The boy went to the store.

My little brother, Jorge, ran to Kenney's Candy Store on the corner of Monroe to buy his favorite candy, "Yummybears."

—*Jesus*

3. The book is interesting.

Love Story *is a book about two people caring for each other, mostly through the way they act, not by what they say.*

—*Eileen*

4. Some people like to fight.

Fights will break out from time to time whether we like it or not. I just hope all parties would understand that fighting doesn't solve or prevent anything; it only causes more problems.

—Jerry

5. My dad works at the shelter.

My dad works at the local shelter for the homeless where he helps people by giving them food and a warm, safe place to sleep.

—Elizabeth

6. The pitcher threw the ball.

Slowly, the pitcher stretched, lifted his left leg, and brought the ball home to his catcher with a "pop."

—Marcos

7. The people walked across the street.

Cautiously, pedestrians crossed the busy intersection at Miles and Monroe.

—Chris

8. My baby is crying.

Brenda, my one-month-old daughter, cried softly on my arm.

—Maria

9. The book is interesting.

The American literature book brings to life the characters of the past in such stories as "The Outcasts of Poker Flat," written by Brett Harte.

—Jason

10. The house is big.

The huge, rambling house at the top of the hill on 39th Street stands desolate in the moonlight after the throat-slashed body of Paul Riviera was removed earlier in the day.

—Eric

11. The table broke.

The old damaged Victorian table creaked as it crumbled to the floor.

—*Maria*

Below is an example of journalistic writing, where the writer has answered questions about *who, what, where, when, why, how,* and *how much* to create interest:

At 10 P.M., Friday evening, a crazed man broke into the Hearst Castle, abducting Patty Hearst, daughter of William Randolph Hearst, Jr. She was having a slumber party with four of her classmates. Security officers were baffled by the suddenness of the girl's disappearance and were not divulging any speculation as to how the man was able to elude security and enter the bedroom window of the mansion.

The Hearsts have appeared on TV, pleading for the release of their daughter. None of the other girls were harmed in the incident.

Many speculate the kidnapping was a mere demonstration of power by terrorists to show William Randolph Hearst that they can and will successfully strike at anytime. Hearst Castle representatives had no comment regarding the speculation.

Meanwhile, the FBI is employing the use of dogs and helicopters in an all-out effort to find the victim of this shocking crime.

—*David*

5. *Recommended Exercises*

Copy the sterile sentences from the examples above and have students "dress up" the simple subject–predicate–object sentences to create their own versions.

Students can bring a newspaper article to class and study how the writer answers the journalistic questions "who," "what," etc. in the opening paragraph. Following the opening paragraph, the students can study how the writer develops his or her story around those same questions.

Courtroom Approach to Writing

The courtroom approach to writing is simple and effective. It imitates what happens in the courtroom. First, there is the "charge."

Example: *Murder in the first degree.*

Next, there is the presentation of the "evidence."

Example: *The murder weapon.*

Finally, there is a "verdict" rendered.

Example: *Guilty or not guilty.*

One advantage of the courtroom approach is that it sets out a clear beginning, middle, and end. The "charge" should be short and to the point. The "evidence" may be as many sentences as needed to prove the case. Each paragraph may contain three or more sentences, whatever is appropriate. The "verdict" is a wrap-up sentence that relates specifically to the "charge," includes the consequences, and summarizes the outcome.

Most of the required writing exercises that students will do can fit easily into "The Courtroom Approach."

Daily Lesson Plan

1. *Writing Lab (8–10 minutes)*

The Writing Lab consists of giving the students *three* separate topics from the list in Chapter 13. These topics and questions have proven to be sure-fire writing starters. The students should write for about eight to ten minutes to complete the three paragraphs.

Hint: Tell the students to place a check next to the paragraph they consider to be their best writing. Ask the students to use examples whenever possible.

2. *Spelling (5 minutes)*

On the back of the Writing Lab paper, quiz the students on ten words from a list of "Most Commonly Misspelled Words." The students should correct their own papers and keep an account of their own spelling progress. Allow them approximately five minutes to complete the quiz.

3. *Grammar (12 minutes)*

The teacher may choose any good grammar workbook and have the students do one or two exercises on any topic that has proven to be a trouble spot for the class. The students should be allowed approximately twelve minutes to complete this exercise.

4. *Lesson for the Day: The Courtroom Approach to Writing (with Recommended Exercises, 30 minutes)*

The following example paragraphs show a definite beginning, middle, and end. The concluding sentence should refer back to the opening statement.

The facilities at Penguin Park in North Seaside are inadequate. The restrooms have been indecently tagged and are incredibly filthy. The playground swings are old and unsafe, and the slides have sharp metal corners that tear little fingers and toes. There are no flowers in the park, and the grass on the unleveled field is dry and ugly. I cannot let my children play at an unsafe and inadequate park. I wish the city of Seaside would correct the problems at Penguin Park.

—Chris

Summer will soon be here. And with it the scorching sun that drives everybody under water at Jackson Pool. Whining air conditioners will fill the neighborhood with their incessant racket. Little children will run through backyard sprinklers, yelping and screaming with delight. Parents, heavy with sweat, will return home from a long day's work. Yes, summer is just around the corner. Isn't it great?

—Jimmy

Houseplants bring life and freshness to a room. Their life and growth make us feel alive. That may be because the oxygen they create in the room is healthy for our lungs and blood. Plants are not only healthy to have around, but they are beautiful and make our houses warm and fresh.

—Maria

Getting older brings with it many responsibilities. No longer do we take for granted the food that is served us nor the table upon which it is served. And somehow we learn that clothes don't just appear in our closets; they are purchased with hard earned money. The very lights we read by, the water we drink, and the washer/dryer that keeps us fresh and clean are all necessities that are bought at a great price. Add to these expenses countless others; for instance, cars, repairs, and insurance. Getting older is not just aging. It is maturing and assuming responsibilities.

—Jerry

Easter break was worth waiting for. My sister-in-law, Terri, and her friend, Jean, both gourmet cooks, drove out from Denver. My favorite niece from San Diego popped over for a few days, and another friend of the family decided to spend the holiday with us. When everybody—kids, boyfriends, and all— finally gathered for Easter dinner, there were fifteen of us to enjoy the ham, pies, gourmet vegetable dishes, and salads. While the food and champagne added to the festivities, the real joy was generated by having us all together again. Now, that's what I call a real Easter break!

—Cruz

The facilities at Penguin Park in North Indio are totally inadequate. There are no restrooms and no benches in the park. The trees provide little shade or beauty. As for the basketball courts, they are littered with broken glass, the baskets are bent, and the backboards are filled with graffiti. As you can see, the park is in bad shape.

—Jimmy

Christmas will soon be here. The sound of Christmas carols and bells will fill the air, and the sweet scent of pine needles will linger in the streets. The houses, decorated in lights and wreaths, will be complete with the aroma of baked pumpkin pies and gingerbread cookies. Family and friends will come together and share their joy and presents. I can hardly wait for the Christmas season to come.

—Elizabeth

Stater Bros. is a great place to work. The store is in town and not too far from my house. The people who work there help you understand your job and teach you to help customers with their bags. I give myself a lot of credit for getting a job at such a good store.

—Jimmy

Smart people buy old cars. For one thing, the older cars are easier to work on and are inexpensive to repair. A person can buy an older car for about a thousand dollars or less. Old cars look nice when they are fixed up and detailed out. I wouldn't mind having a 1964 Impala today. Old cars are not only fun to work on, but they are inexpensive to operate, too. I'll never buy a new car so long as there are old T-Birds, Impalas, and Regals around.

—Vincent

The sun and the moon are like brother and sister. The sun and moon are like siblings because they are always in competition over the sky. The moon is usually jealous of how bright the sun is, so he brags about his army of stars. The sun brings energy and heat, while the moon is soothing and tranquil. The sun and moon are like brother and sister, and the earth is their mother.

—Tianna

5. *Recommended Exercises*

Write ten short sentences that can be easily developed by using the courtroom approach. Have each student expand one or two of those sentences into a complete paragraph. As with all the exercises, they may flow into a homework assignment.

3

Enumeration

If one looks closely, one can almost see the word "number" in the approach to writing called "enumeration." Enumeration is simply telling your audience that you will discuss several things. This is probably the easiest way for beginning writers to get started.

Special connective words are employed when using this approach. Words like *first, second, third, next, after that, then,* and *finally.*

For further clarification, study the examples in the "Lesson for the Day."

Daily Lesson Plan

1. *Writing Lab (8–10 minutes)*

The Writing Lab consists of giving the students *three* separate topics from the list in Chapter 13. These topics and questions have proven to be sure-fire writing starters. The students should write for about eight to ten minutes to complete the three paragraphs.

Hint: Tell the students to place a check next to the paragraph they consider to be their best writing. Ask the students to use examples whenever possible.

2. *Spelling (5 minutes)*

On the back of the Writing Lab paper, quiz the students on ten words from a list of "Most Commonly Misspelled Words." The students should correct their own papers and keep an account of their own spelling progress. Allow them approximately five minutes to complete the quiz.

3. *Grammar (12 minutes)*

The teacher may choose any good grammar workbook and have the students do one or two exercises on any topic that has proven to be a trouble spot for the class. The students should be allowed approximately twelve minutes to complete this exercise.

4. *Lesson for the Day: Enumeration (with Recommended Exercises, 30 minutes)*

The easiest way to write a paragraph is to number or list the topics about which the student is interested in writing. This is referred to as development by means of *enumeration*. Start with a short sentence that indicates that several descriptive references will be written about the topic.

Examples:

Penguin Park needs some improving.

Let me tell you what I did today.

Try to join the developing ideas by using *first, then, finally, to begin with, following that, in conclusion*, or similar transitional words.

Study the following paragraphs that are developed by means of *enumeration*:

> There are several things about the new recreation center I would like to share with you. The playground, for example, has a slide, swing, and plenty of sand around it to play in. The center also has a very nice track upstairs, where people can run, jog, and walk. While you jog, you can watch people play basketball in the downstairs gym. There are about six courts to play on. The center also has a weight room with all different kinds of weight systems. Finally, there are two racquetball court rooms, located near the weight room.
>
> —Lisa

> I'll teach you how to prepare the baby's formula. First, you have to sterilize the nipples; and while you're sterilizing the nipples, you may start preparing the baby's formula. You begin by measuring one scoop of powdered milk and pouring it into the bottle. Then, you add two ounces of water into the bottle.

Finally, you may remove the nipples from the pan in which you sterilized them, replace the bottle top onto the bottle, and shake it before you give it to the baby. Now you know how to make the baby's formula.

—Maria

I'll tell you how my mom makes enchiladas that are good enough to die for. To begin with, she uses the choicest ground meat available. Then, she slowly simmers the meat until it is tender and juicy. Next, she fries our favorite Bell Tortillas in a metal pan and makes them soft. When the tortillas are soft, she adds the tomato sauce to the meat. My mom then rolls each tortilla like a taquito. Finally, the Wisconsin cheddar cheese is sprinkled over the taquitos, and they are placed in the oven. I just can't wait until the next time my mom makes Enchiladas de Juarez.

—Elizabeth

I did a few necessary things today. Arising about seven, I dressed, ate, and took my brother and sister to school in my new '68 VW. After that, I cleaned my car inside and out. Finally, and most importantly, I visited for a long time with Linda, my girlfriend of two weeks. It was a most pleasant day.

—Jimmy

I disliked several things about the Date Festival. To begin with, there were too many people attending at one time. The crowd was just too big. Another thing I disliked was the outrageous noise of the crowd and the games. The last thing that I disliked about the festival, was the outrageous prices for food, drinks, and rides. All in all, the fair was one big rip-off.

—Marcos

5. Recommended Exercises

Write ten sentences that could be developed into paragraphs by means of enumeration. Have students write paragraphs using two sentences of their choice. Again, these exercises may be given as a homework assignment.

4

Questions/Topic Sentences

Questions provide the students with sure-fire writing starters. They are thought-provoking and enable the students to express their thoughts without being intimidated. Questions enable the students to explore new writing skills and examine their feelings regarding the issue raised by the question.

The topic sentence, which students have the most difficulty developing, will generally be the first sentence after the question. For example, the question, "How do you feel about cigarette smoking?" would be followed by the topic sentence, "I think cigarette smoking is not only harmful to one's health but is also a disgusting and dirty habit."

Following the topic sentence in the example, the student will find it quite easy to develop the paragraph using either the "courtroom" or the "enumeration" approach.

Through the use of questions, writing a paragraph becomes easy for the student. Before long, questions are not needed as a tool for developing topic sentences and paragraphs. But for the time being, questions do help students to start writing and, quite frankly, to enjoy it.

Daily Lesson Plan

1. *Writing Lab (8–10 minutes)*
   The Writing Lab consists of giving the students *three* separate topics from the list in Chapter 13. These topics and questions have proven to be sure-fire writing starters. The students should write for about eight to ten minutes to complete the three paragraphs.

Hint: Tell the students to place a check next to the paragraph they consider to be their best writing. Ask the students to use examples whenever possible.

2. *Spelling (5 minutes)*

On the back of the Writing Lab paper, quiz the students on ten words from a list of "Most Commonly Misspelled Words." The students should correct their own papers and keep an account of their own spelling progress. Allow them approximately five minutes to complete the quiz.

3. *Grammar (12 minutes)*

The teacher may choose any good grammar workbook and have the students do one or two exercises on any topic that has proven to be a trouble spot for the class. The students should be allowed approximately twelve minutes to complete this exercise.

4. *Lesson for the Day: Questions/Topic Sentences (with Recommended Exercises, 30 minutes)*

Use questions that refer to thoughts, feelings and life experiences such as "What do you really like to do?" "How do you feel about cigarette smoking?" or "What is your favorite present and why?" Below are examples of paragraphs developed from questions:

There is something I really like to do. This something is going to the Knights game with my dad. It is really enjoyable and I get a chance to bond with him. We have no boys in my family, so I know it is hard for my dad to bond with us. My sister and I are growing up and I can see the sadness in him. I try my hardest not to grow up too fast and I always try to be my "Daddy's Little Girl."

—Laura

Cigarette smoking can be dangerous to your social life because it is disgusting. The smell of stale burnt tobacco on your breath is a real turnoff, no matter how good looking you are. The aroma of your last stogy lingers on your face, in your hair, on your clothes, and on your friends. So, if you find yourself alone more than you like, wake up and smell the ashes. Smoking is dangerous to your social life.

—Vince

My favorite present of all time is my skateboard. It is a gift that gives me pleasure every day. I have learned from working on it how to repair the pieces. I have also met many good people while riding it. My skateboard is a gift that keeps on giving.

—Vincent

I have had no day I would like to forget. I have learned from every bad or unpleasant experience. On the contrary, I want to remember every day and every experience. Perhaps, by remembering, I can avoid making the same mistakes over again. Forgetting is a form of denial. I am here to learn.

—Vince

There was a time I said something I didn't mean. I said something to my friend to put her down. I knew I didn't mean it when I saw the hurt in her eyes. Why did I say that? I thought I was making a joke. Jokes made at the expense of other people's feelings are not funny.

—Barbarosa

The sporks at a local fast food restaurant really bother me! Dwelling somewhere between the world of forks and spoons are the sporks. Sporks are neither round enough to hold a complete spoonful of liquid nor sharp enough to fork a good mouthful of salad. These instruments are medieval torture. It is enough to remove one's trust in the ever-faithful spoon when I cut my tongue trying to lick up every last drop of ice cream.

—Vincent

Everybody has a turning point in his life. I'm no different. The first day of high school was great. I met new people. I started to play football and signed up for other sports. A year later, I found new friends that liked to party and have a good time. Then I started to get into trouble. Now I realize that I was doing wrong. I was following the wrong people. These "friends" were involved with the wrong things. The sophomore year in high school was my turning point.

—Chris

I would like to relive my tenth grade year. I had everything going for me that year. I was still in school. My dad had bought me a new car. Once I had the car, I thought I could do anything and go anywhere I wanted. Later on that year my dad found out I had too many people in the car and I wasn't going to school. He took the car away from me. If I could relive this time, I would know what not to do and I would still be in school. For example, I wouldn't have more than three people in the car at a time. I would try not to ditch school, and I would try to listen to my dad. If only I could relive that year, I could look back and see success in school and in athletics. And, by the way, I'd be driving my car to school each day and to all the games and dances.

—Jimmy

When I have children, I will teach them to be thankful for what they have and to be polite and courteous to others. I'll teach them that money can't buy happiness, and it is more important to have less but be happy than to have more but be unhappy. Instead of being selfish and greedy, I'd teach them to help others who are in need by donating things to Goodwill or the Salvation Army, and to treat others the way they want to be treated.

—Christie

I'm really concerned about my cat. I think she's retarded. She falls out of trees, and when birds fly by the window, she forgets the glass is there and jumps anyway. This may come from my little sister, who hugs her and squeezes her constantly. I think this may cut off the oxygen to her brain or something. Once she fell down the stairs and nearly broke her leg. Aren't cats supposed to land on their feet? I'm really concerned about my cat.

—Alec

A time I said something I didn't mean was when I told my mom that I hated her. She makes me really upset sometimes and I say things I don't mean. I'll call her names or tell her I wish she were dead. After I calm down, I usually regret this. But I think my mom knows I didn't mean what I said. I think she knows that I love her.

— Raquel

I'd go to Tokyo, Japan, because I have been there before and loved it. The food is superior, the shops are cool, and you feel pretty safe there. I also have many relatives that live in Japan. My uncle is the head of the Grand Church in Tokyo, and he said that anytime we were in town, we could stay at the church. I'd visit the Daibutsu statue, the deer parks in Nara, the majestic Mount Fuji, Tokyo Tower; and I'd take the bullet train, Shinkansen, *all over Japan. I'd visit the shrines and temples, and learn about the old buildings and civilization. I would want to go during the summer because that is when* Kodomo oyliba *takes place. It is a celebration that lasts the whole summer. Kids in school bands play cheerful music as they walk around the church. "Ocha Doozoln!" When translated into English, this means, "There is some tea!" Other church clubs hand out barley tea to tourists and townspeople who pass by. Everyone is in the mood for this lovely summer festival. At the end of each day of* Kodomo oyliba, *bright fireworks are lit behind the Grand Church for all to see. When I was in Japan, my favorite sight was the fireworks at* Kodomo oyliba. *This is what makes Tokyo my kind of town.*

— Christie

When I lived in Garner Valley two winters ago, I shot a bluebird with my pellet gun. When I came up to the bird, it was still alive. I put the bird out of its misery by shooting it one more time — this time in the head. After shooting the bluebird, I felt pretty bad. I felt heartless and wished that God would forgive me for destroying one of His little creatures. That very day I made myself a promise that if God would forgive me I would never again kill a bluebird.

— Joe

The boy I marry will be beautiful on the inside. I am not very picky about what he looks like, but he must be cute. I am going to have to marry him and spend my life with him. He will have to love children, because I want a huge family. I want a big house with lots of people in it. Finally, we must be in love. I want to marry for love, not money or some of the other reasons that people get married. He will respect my decisions and stand by me no matter what the result might be, and I will do the same for him.

—Sydney

The biggest surprise of my life was being born. I didn't expect it and had no prior warning. There I was, kicking back in the womb, and wham! I'm sliding downward and I'm really confused. A couple pushes and I'm in an overly lit room being held by a blue man. Smack! I get my first spanking and I cry. It was a frightful surprise, but it was worth it.

—Tianna

I'm not very good at algebra. I despise it! I've always had a hard time with math, but this year especially. I failed almost five tests, and I had to go in every morning for three weeks to be tutored. Fortunately, I'm going to take it again this year, but I'm afraid I'll always struggle with it and I'll fail again. There is something about algebraic equations that makes my head want to explode, and that is what I am not good at.

—Christie

My heroine is a woman, a queen. She walks with every step upon rose petals, golden dust flying at her heels. The flaming sun upon her sweet caramel skin, her mind sharp, her thoughts thick. Sweet smelling breezes whirl through her raven black hair. Her eyes bright, you can see golden spears and silver waterfalls looping, soaring, doubling, and somersaulting in her dark brown eyes. The sun in her smile. Her heart is big and full of love.

Her life hasn't always been easy. She hasn't always been wearing silk robes, walking on golden mats. Rising to the top in a male-dominated world, she persevered and now her high, sharp cries resound like thunderbolts in servants' ears. She rose to the top, but not without pain. The loss was a love, her glass-like tears forever sounding in her heart.

But the last year brought joy and happiness, a son. She's protective, folding her arms gently around her sleeping child. Her soul shining brightly like a diamond in the sky, you can still see her shadow upon the moon. She is bigger than all emotion. She faced, struggled, and overcame all odds that still face women today. Cleopatra is and always will be my heroine.

—Krystle

5. Recommended Exercises

Ask the students to write ten questions that could be developed into paragraphs. Then have them use some of those questions to write a few paragraphs. Use this recommendation for a homework assignment as well.

Starting Sentences

Variety is a crucial element of writing because it reduces boredom. Nowhere is variety more effective than in the first word of each sentence. Beginning a sentence with an "ing" word is one way to do that. Frankly, I prefer starting a sentence with an "ly" word. Full, musical sentences may start with two adjectives. There are also other ways to provide variety in sentence starts such as the use of apposition, prepositional phrases and clauses, et cetera.

In this lesson, we will explore a variety of ways to begin sentences. Meanwhile, the students should work to develop their sentences to provide that crucial element, *variety*.

Daily Lesson Plan

1. *Writing Lab (8–10 minutes)*

The Writing Lab consists of giving the students *three* separate topics from the list in Chapter 13. These topics and questions have proven to be sure-fire writing starters. The students should write for about eight to ten minutes to complete the three paragraphs.

Hint: Tell the students to place a check next to the paragraph they consider to be their best writing. Ask the students to use examples whenever possible.

2. *Spelling (5 minutes)*

On the back of the Writing Lab paper, quiz the students on ten words from a list of "Most Commonly Misspelled Words." The students should correct their own papers and keep an account of their own spelling progress. Allow them approximately five minutes to complete the quiz.

3. *Grammar (12 minutes)*

The teacher may choose any good grammar workbook and have the students do one or two exercises on any topic that has proven to be a trouble spot for the class. The students should be allowed approximately twelve minutes to complete this exercise.

4. *Lesson for the Day: Starting Sentences (with Recommended Exercises, 30 minutes)*

Practice starting sentences in a variety of ways.

Try to begin the sentence with an "ing" word: *Laughing children play together along the seashore.* And *Burning logs quietly crumble into ashes in the open pit.*

Try to begin a sentence with an "ly" word: *Lonely, homeless people line up in front of the shelter for a bologna sandwich and a bowl of hot chicken soup.* Or *Slowly and calmly, Pam called the police when a stranger was in her house.*

Try to begin a sentence with two adjectives: *Cold, bitter winds blow through the dark cemetery.* Or *Strong, tall lifeguards flirt openly with bikini clad girls on the beach.*

Try to begin the first sentence of a paragraph with: *At first . . .*

Try to begin the second sentence with: *Then, . . .*

Try to begin the third sentence with: *Finally, . . .*

Try to start a sentence with a 'when' preposition: *Yesterday, Tomorrow, Annually, Last year,* etc.

Try to start a sentence with an apposition: George, the *postman, . . . ,* My *favorite caddy, Bebe Eyes, . . .* and so on.

The following paragraphs demonstrate the strategies explained above:

Cold, bitter winds blow through the dark cemetery. Tombstones scattered in the graveyard cast devilish shadows in the night. A wolf howls somewhere in the light-deprived distance. *The ground starts to tremble and there is another howl, but this time it's not the wolf. White bleached bones emerge from the ground, standing by their own free will. Something strange is going down at the cemetery, but what can you expect, it's All Hallows Eve.*

—*Jason*

Dancing, the warrior avoided powerful attacks. He is Ninja and must play with honor. The attacker is an ugly brute. He's large, muscular, and powerful, but slow. The Ninja turns and pivots, then lets loose with a side kick, catching Mr. Ugly in the mid-section. Then, the Ninja ducks and spins, extending his leg for a sweep. The big man gets caught and falls to the floor with a large thump. The battle is won. The Ninja is triumphant.

—*Jason*

"It's worth trying," said a drug dealer on the street. At first I had no clue what he was talking about. Then he brought out a needle, and I realized where he was coming from.

—*Antonio*

5. *Recommended Exercises*

Ask students to write ten sentences, all of which begin a different way, as shown in the examples. As time permits, have students develop these sentences into paragraphs. Continue this exercise into a homework assignment.

6

The Use of *However* and *Therefore*

This simple technique is worth practicing. Its framework has been used to produce superior writing, some of which follows in this chapter. There are, perhaps, many other models that can be used to direct the student's thinking in such a way as to produce a logical, clear, and forceful paragraph, but this formula has proven to be very successful.

The first sentence in this paragraph begins with a short statement. The second sentence begins with *However*. The last sentence begins with *Therefore*.

Daily Lesson Plan

1. *Writing Lab (8–10 minutes)*

The Writing Lab consists of giving the students *three* separate topics from the list in Chapter 13. These topics and questions have proven to be sure-fire writing starters. The students should write for about eight to ten minutes to complete the three paragraphs.

Hint: Tell the students to place a check next to the paragraph they consider to be their best writing. Ask the students to use examples whenever possible.

2. *Spelling (5 minutes)*

On the back of the Writing Lab paper, quiz the students on ten words from a list of "Most Commonly Misspelled Words." The students should correct their own papers and keep an account of their own spelling progress. Allow them approximately five minutes to complete the quiz.

3. *Grammar (12 minutes)*

The teacher may choose any good grammar workbook and have the students do one or two exercises on any topic that has proven to be a trouble spot for the class. The students should be allowed approximately twelve minutes to complete this exercise.

4. *Lesson for the Day: The Use of* However *and* Therefore *(with Recommended Exercises, 30 minutes)*

The students should begin their paragraph with a short sentence, then start the second sentence with *However.* Finally, the last sentence should begin with *Therefore.*

The paragraphs below demonstrate the however/therefore technique.

I parked my new car in the driveway. However, when I began to think about the payments, insurance, repairs, and the cost of gasoline, I had second thoughts about my new purchase. Therefore, after analyzing all aspects of the deal, I decided to return the car to the dealership within the seventy-two hour trial period.

—Chris

I went out and bought myself a new car. However, it didn't look nice when I parked it in the driveway. The tires were too big, and it didn't have chrome rims. It looked like a family car, and I wanted something sporty. Therefore, I replaced the tires with smaller ones and added deep-dish chrome rims.

—Jimmy

Fog rolled into the Northern Valley yesterday morning. However, when I got up to have breakfast, I noticed that the fog was beginning to disappear. The sun was warming the atmosphere and causing the fog to slowly fade away. By 9:30 A.M. the fog had disappeared and the sun was shining brightly. Therefore, the early morning fog doesn't make me unhappy because I know it won't last too long.

—Elizabeth

All day long it has looked as though it would rain. However, not a single drop has fallen. Rain is something very rare and beautiful in the desert. We need more rain here than in other places in this country. Therefore, I wouldn't mind if it rained in the desert more often than it generally does.

—Jeffrey

The Surgeon General has stated that cigarette smoking is bad for one's health. However, this warning doesn't seem to be bothering the cigarette smokers. Reports also say that cigarette smoke is even worse for the non-smoker than for the smoker. Therefore, I would suggest that cigarette smokers stop smoking in public. Better yet, stop smoking altogether.

—Raquel

5. *Recommended Exercises*

Have students write ten short sentences and practice using *however* and *therefore* to develop several paragraphs. Do some of this exercise for homework.

7

Connectives (Transitionals)

One cannot overemphasize the importance of the proper use of connectives. Consequently, it is nearly impossible to write logical, clear, and wholesome themes without them. Furthermore, a theme holds together one's writing in its entirety when the proper connective is used.

Daily Lesson Plan

1. *Writing Lab (8–10 minutes)*

The Writing Lab consists of giving the students *three* separate topics from the list in Chapter 13. These topics and questions have proven to be sure-fire writing starters. The students should write for about eight to ten minutes to complete the three paragraphs.

Hint: Tell the students to place a check next to the paragraph they consider their best writing. Ask the students to use examples whenever possible.

2. *Spelling (5 minutes)*

On the back of the Writing Lab paper, quiz the students on ten words from a list of "Most Commonly Misspelled Words." The students should correct their own papers and keep an account of their own spelling progress. Allow them approximately five minutes to complete the quiz.

3. *Grammar (12 minutes)*

The teacher may choose any good grammar workbook and have the students do one or two exercises on any topic that has

proven to be a trouble spot for the class. The students should be allowed approximately twelve minutes to complete this exercise.

4. *Lesson for the Day: Connectives (with Recommended Exercises, 30 minutes)*

By now the students should have in hand their own list of transitional words. These can be gathered from any grammar book.

Sample connectives: *for instance, also, in addition to, moreover, in spite of, on the other hand, first, second, finally, least important, as a result, for this reason,* etc.

Study the examples given below; then have students complete the following sample sentences:

All soldiers are expected to participate in combat. Of course . . .

Politics in the country must cease. In short . . .

We speak openly of the fears we have for Mother Earth. Yet . . .

A rainbow is an interesting phenomenon. What's more . . .

Learning golf etiquette is a necessity. First . . .

Kids under fourteen are not given work permits. Nevertheless . . .

Going to college is a test in economic survival. In fact . . .

Some folks find it awkward to speak in public. For example . . .

The campus needs to be kept clean. Consequently . . .

The following sentences demonstrate the use of transitional words:

> *Kids under fourteen are not given work permits. However, they can get a job babysitting for a neighbor or relative.*
>
> —*Alex*

> *Some people find it awkward to speak in front of a crowd. For example, when kids are asked to recite their poems for the class or for parents, they often lose their place or hesitate.*
>
> —*Lisa*

The campus needs to be kept clean. Therefore, I'm asking my classmates to participate in cleaning up the campus whenever there is a need to pick up trash.

—*David*

Some people find it awkward to speak in front of a group. For example, my friend, Roland, was so nervous he almost fainted. But he calmed down and did his best. The teacher ended up giving him a good grade.

—*Tito*

Martha is talking on the phone; she's conversing with a friend about her personal life. As a matter of fact, Martha is always talking on the phone, and her first topic is her personal life.

—*Maria*

My daughter is sleeping this morning because she didn't sleep well last night. As a matter of fact, she generally picks the day hours to sleep and the night hours to be awake.

—*Cruz*

All soldiers are expected to participate in combat. Of course, there are exceptions. Soldiers with physical problems cannot do some of the challenging jobs that the average soldier can do. And women are limited to certain physically-suited jobs.

—*Eric*

5. *Recommended Exercises*

Have students develop several paragraphs using the topic sentences in the examples given above. Make sure they choose the correct transitional to start the second sentence. Then do several paragraphs for homework.

8

Descriptions

Descriptive writing does not just happen. It is carefully arranged to be logical as well as poetic. It uses comparisons, similes, and metaphors to make the description more musical and colorful.

However, along with the colorful words and metaphors, there is a very distinct, logical order that is followed. For example, if a person is to be described, one might begin by describing his hair and continue on with his face, shoulders, torso, legs and feet, and so on, from top to bottom.

The following exercise has been quite successful when introducing descriptive writing. Have the students write a paragraph consisting of three sentences. The first sentence should begin with "Before me . . . ," followed by the second sentence starting with "To the right . . ." and finally, the last sentence beginning with "Above . . . ."

Daily Lesson Plan

1. *Writing Lab (8–10minutes)*

The Writing Lab consists of giving the students *three* separate topics from the list in Chapter 13. These topics and questions have proven to be sure-fire writing starters. The students should write for about eight to ten minutes to complete the three paragraphs.

Hint: Tell the students to place a check next to the paragraph they consider to be their best writing. Ask the students to use examples whenever possible.

2. *Spelling (5 minutes)*

On the back of the Writing Lab paper, quiz the students on ten words from a list of "Most Commonly Misspelled Words." The students should correct their own papers and keep an account of their own spelling progress. Allow them approximately five minutes to complete the quiz.

3. *Grammar (12 minutes)*

The teacher may choose any good grammar workbook and have the students do one or two exercises on any topic that has proven to be a trouble spot for the class. The students should be allowed approximately twelve minutes to complete this exercise.

4. *Lesson for the Day: Descriptions (with Recommended Exercises, 30 minutes)*

The following examples show good descriptive writing:

Before her is a young girl with a look of hunger and discomfort. To the right is a younger child crying tears of fear and unwantedness. Above is the sky, and she is asking for God's help.

—Eileen

Before me stood a majestic statue of the Greek mythological god, Zeus. To the right was a ravenous, bloodthirsty Rottweiler with bloodshot eyes. It stared into my soul, conscious of my trespassing. Above was a castle towering over trees that thrived on the hillside.

—Tito

Before me was a little Dutch house. It was white with a yellow-trimmed roof that created a type of awning. It had two windows divided in four sections. The short door was decorated with hearts. To my right there was a large brown windmill, blowing about an April breeze. Tulips lined the cobblestone walkway, and children ran through the street, skipping and singing. Above, a royal blue sky embraced the flat Dutch countryside.

—Krystle

Before me was an enormous round table with a beautiful arrangement of roses in the center. To the right stood my mom in a white dress, anxiously waiting to serve the dinner. Above, there was the ceiling with Chinese decoration and a beautiful golden lamp which gave light in the room.

—*Elizabeth*

Before him there is the sea relentlessly hitting the rocks and breaking, sending a spray of white foam into the air. To the right is a cold wall of solid rock rising up as high as the eye can see. Above, bleak thunderclouds threaten to ruin the rest of the day.

—*Eric*

Before them is a beautiful new sports car with chrome wheels and tan interior. To the right of them were the popular game show host, Pat Sajak, and his lovely assistant, Vanna White. They are the stars of the ever-popular late night game show Wheel of Fortune. *Above them were the blinding studio lights all shining in their direction.*

—*Eric*

Before me was a giant mountain, standing with its huge, beautiful figure and bringing life to the marvelous landscape. To the right of me and continuing below was a wide river with its strong currents making the water clean and bringing freshness to the area. Above the river, the jungle was alive with wild birds and beasts.

—*Maria*

Before her stood the man of her dreams. He was tall, dark, and had big, beautiful brown eyes. To the right of her was the bench where she remembers he first kissed her. Above her were the stars and moonlight shining, as they held each other tightly in their arms.

—*Candace*

Before me lay a bare and desolate desert, the sand stretching out for miles. All I could think about was my thirst and hunger. I lost track of how many hours I had been roaming the desert. Each step I took, my feet became heavier. To the right of me was what I thought was a hotel, but I later found out when I had walked to it that it was a dreamlike mirage. Above, circling overhead, were vultures waiting for my imminent demise.

—Curtis

Before me I see the eternal, flaming pits of Hell. To the right I see a shadowy figure holding a long crooked blade. As I look into the eyes of this creature I see nothing but darkness. Above me are the beautifully decorated gates to Heaven, close enough to look at yet far out of my reach, for it is much too late to recover from my sins.

—Antonio

Before me is a large round vase. In it, there are some colorful green and purple grapes. There are also some yellow pears and some red apples. To the right is a small table with a glass top. Resting on the glass top is a vase of beautiful pink and violet flowers. Above is a shiny brass chandelier with twelve small antique lights.

—Elizabeth

5. Recommended Exercises

Ask the student to describe an action or a place by using "Before me . . . ," "To the right . . . ," and "Above . . . ," as shown above.

The location can be any familiar place, i.e., a hospital waiting room, a lunch line, a TV room, a classroom, et cetera. As always, the exercises can be added to the homework assignment.

9

Spatials/Vignettes

Spatial has to do with the five senses: hearing, seeing, touching, tasting, and smelling. The spatial exercises that follow are self-explanatory. One simply describes three things about each of the five senses.

In working with vignettes (little "slices of life"), the tendency is to put oneself into the story. However, the key is to describe the so-called "slice of life" by reporting only what one might see, hear, touch, taste, or smell without the use of words such as "I," "me," "my," "he," "she," or "they."

The small sapphire flame whispered in the hearth. (correct format)

I could feel the warmth of the small sapphire flame as it whispered in the hearth. (incorrect format.)

Note: Have the students study the difference in the examples on the following pages.

Daily Lesson Plan

1. *Writing Lab (8–10 minutes)*

The writing lab consists of giving the students *three* separate topics from the list in Chapter 13. These topics and questions have proven to be sure-fire writing starters. The students should write for about eight to ten minutes to complete the three paragraphs.

Hint: Tell the students to place a check next to the paragraph they consider to be their best writing. Ask the students to use examples whenever possible.

2. *Spelling (5 minutes)*

On the back of the Writing Lab paper, quiz the students on ten words from the list of "Most Commonly Misspelled Words." The students should correct their own papers and keep an account of their spelling progress. Allow them approximately five minutes to complete the quiz.

3. *Grammar (12 minutes)*

The teacher may choose any good grammar workbook and have the students do one or two exercises on any topic that has proven to be a trouble spot for the class. The students should be allowed approximately twelve minutes to complete this exercise.

4. *Lesson for the Day: Spatials/Vignettes (with Recommended Exercises, 30 minutes)*

Have the students write three separate spatials/vignettes. Each paragraph should describe one of the five different senses.

Spatial examples:

Her hair is beautiful like threads that weave life. Her eyes could light the world and are more beautiful than a meadow. Her face could give peace to the world and end all hate.

—Josh

The pounding of the ocean commanding its legions of waves echoed in ears. The sudden screaming of a comet sliced through the night. The few remaining gulls squawked among themselves over remnants of food.

—Krystle

The flower's petals felt like raw silk. The warm grass tickled the bare feet. The rough bark of the tree felt strong and harsh.

—Krystle

At first the rain was softly tapping on the windows. Then it began to come down at a faster pace and started to rattle the chimes and window sills. Finally the clouds broke, and we had a full thunder and lightning storm.

—Heidi

The fresh morning dew on the hillside sends its clean scent into the valley below. The fragrance of spring flowers hovers in the mountain air. The musky smell of the trees is overwhelming.

—*Krystle*

Vignettes ("Slices of Life") examples:

Note: These "word pictures" or "images" are written in the third person. Keep yourself out of the description.

Deep red wine flowed elegantly from the crystal serving pitcher into the fancy silver goblet.

—*Elizabeth*

Huge waves crash onto the white sandy beach. Seagulls fly toward the sun as it melts into the great blue ocean. Scattered white clouds lace the sky with beauty.

—*Eric*

Wildflowers, daisies, dandelions, and lupine grow carelessly in the grassy field as in a forgotten flower garden.

—*Eileen*

The small sapphire flames whispered in the hearth, and a cherry log crumbled with a tinselly rustle into the open pit.

—*Tom*

The furry calico cat sits upon the fence as if standing guard while a butterfly lands daintily on a yellow flower.

—*Linda*

A rose-colored vapor chases a high-flying jet across a desert landscape. Palm branches interrupt the view of the sun as it melts slowly behind the mountains. Above, in the now dusky sky, a fleet of noisy geese dashes northward for the summer.

—*Jerry*

The enormous sky with puffy white clouds arcs its blue canopy over the green sea. The whitecap waves tumble rhythmically onto the rocky seashore. Children of all sizes stand poised to challenge the full force of the ocean.

— *Eileen*

The red leather booths at Teresa's Mexican Restaurant are teeming with happy families. While children sip their tall orange drinks and pick at their quesadillas, parents and grandparents are riveted in lively conversation. Two waitresses dressed in long floral gowns balance platters of carne asada and salsa as they approach the tables.

— *Elizabeth*

5. *Recommended Exercises*

Have the students write several vignettes describing three things they can see from a particular location. Continue this exercise for a homework assignment.

10

Clustering/Outlining

It is virtually impossible to write longer themes without planning the major steps: *introduction*, *body*, and *conclusion*. For that purpose, *clustering* is a useful tool. Students should brainstorm all aspects of the topic and then put ideas in some kind of order by making a simple outline. Now the student is ready to write.

Daily Lesson Plan

1. *Writing Lab (8–10 minutes)*

The Writing Lab consists of giving the students *three* separate topics from the list in Chapter 13. These topics and questions have proven to be sure-fire writing starters. The students should write for about eight to ten minutes to complete the three paragraphs.

Hint: Tell the students to place a check next to the paragraph they consider to be their best writing. Ask the students to use examples whenever possible.

2. *Spelling (5 minutes)*

On the back of the Writing Lab paper, quiz the students on ten words from the list of "Most Commonly Misspelled Words." The students should correct their own papers and keep an account of their spelling progress. Allow them approximately five minutes to complete the quiz.

3. *Grammar (12 minutes)*

The teacher may choose any good grammar workbook and have the students do one or two exercises on any topic that has

proven to be a trouble spot for the class. The students should be allowed approximately twelve minutes to complete this exercise.

4. *Lesson for the Day: Clustering/Outlining (with Recommended Exercises, 30 minutes)*

Have the students choose a topic, then brainstorm and select three aspects of that topic. Develop these aspects into three paragraphs for the body of the theme.

Note: When writing longer themes, *clustering* and *outlining* are indispensable. *Clustering* is simply brainstorming about a given topic (a word or idea) and then limiting oneself to discussing three ideas springing from that topic.

Examples:

First, give students a topic and have them brainstorm their ideas (clustering).

Topic: Swimming helps people grow.

Clustering:
1. Keeps body fit
2. Teaches discipline
3. Builds self-esteem

Then have the students put their cluster ideas in order and make a simple outline.

Topic: Swimming helps people grow.

Outlining:
    I. Introduction
        A. Pablo Morales—the swimmer
        B. Pablo Morales—the person
    II. Body
        A. Builds self-esteem
        B. Keeps the body fit
        C. Teaches discipline
    III. Conclusion
        A. Pablo Morales—winner of gold medal in Barcelona

B. Pablo Morales—complete athlete—body and soul

Once the students have limited themselves to three main ideas in the body, have them introduce the topic in the introduction.

Example: *When Pablo Morales won the gold medal in Barcelona for the 100 meter butterfly, nobody could possibly have known the total lifetime of commitment it had taken to win.*

Have the students write three paragraphs. In the first (A), they should discuss how swimming builds self-esteem. In the second (B), they should write about how swimming keeps the body fit; and in the third (C), they should discuss how swimming teaches discipline. When listing main ideas, students should start with the second most important and end with the most important. The third most important idea can go in the middle.

Finally, they must add a conclusion that refers back to the introduction. This will give a feeling of closure, completeness.

Example: *Long, lonely hours of morning workouts molded Pablo Morales into a fit, disciplined, and self-confident swimmer. The gold medal won in the 100 meter butterfly was only incidental to his total growth as a human being.*

The following are three samples of short five paragraph themes using this method:

Happiness

Happiness is the one thing in life everyone is searching for. We are all searching for this because it feels so good to be happy.

When I find happiness, it is only for short terms. For example, last year I wanted a video game. I saved up four months' worth of allowances and bought it. I played with it for a while, but now it's grown old and only gets played about once a week.

Another example is when I wanted some popular "Pump" Hi-top shoes. I got the shoes and was happy until the pump broke. I threw the shoes away, because at that point, they were useless.

My longest term of happiness was when I had gotten a brand new bike. It was fun to ride, and it didn't break for three years. It did make me happy for a long time, but I outgrew the bike and the bike is useless.

My search for happiness seems to be a never-ending cycle. Someday I hope I will find the one thing that will make me happy forever.

—*David*

Teddy Bears

I lie down in bed after a long day. Shadows linger on the walls like paintings of ghosts. I am home by myself; my parents have left on a weekend vacation.

Silence hangs in the air like a fist. The feeling that there is another presence in the room looms over me. I start to get frightened. It's a smothering feeling, not knowing where that presence is.

There is a low whining noise, like a banshee, flowing from the corner of my room. The temperature in the room seems to have dropped ten degrees in that instant. The ground starts to rumble. Cracks appear on the floor; light streams through them. The floor falls through, sending a blinding light with it, and out of this nexus a figure emerges.

As the light dims, I am taken aback. Before me stands a huge teddy bear. The bear stands at least eight feet and has the general appearance of a normal teddy bear except for its red glowing eyes. Mr. Furry Bear looks angry and ready to pounce on me.

To this day, I will not forget that bear. He came from another dimension for only one thing, a HUG!!

—*Jason*

Holidays

On my favorite holiday, fireflies become ballerinas, fluttering in the night, the deepest beauty unfolding before you. It's the blooming of lighted roses airbrushed on the sky. Rubies and sapphires seem to magically shower the captivated audience. Is it a fairy tale?

Children, anxious, their eyes set in wide stares as lasers of emerald, royal blue, orange, pink, and purple dance in the sky. Choruses of "oohs!" and "aahs!" fill the night air. Stars twinkle in their illustrious eminence. Charismatic, wild, and sweet, the last river of crystal light sweeps across the sky.

Sometimes I wonder what makes this holiday so special for me. I finally found out it was the time spent on the beaches, splashing water with friends while red flares shot into the night and burst into colorful raindrops.

It also was the smiles and caring, the way it brings together friends and family, the unspoken joy flowing from each heart.

I'm never more amazed by the love on the faces of people than on this holiday. So now I know why I'm the happiest one under the stars on the Fourth of July.

—Krystle

5. Recommended Exercises

Have the students choose a topic and cluster ideas around it. Next, ask them to choose three ideas regarding the topic that they would like to develop.

Now they should put the three ideas into an outline as discussed earlier in the chapter. Finally, have them write a five-paragraph theme. This can be finished for homework.

11

Short Essays

Essays are personal glimpses, interpretations, or ideas about a given topic. Some essays that reveal personal ideas and feelings stem from questions such as: "Was there a day I'd like to forget?" Some are the product of one or two word assignments like "My Hero" or "Happiness."

Some of the essays that follow in the "Lesson for the Day" were the product of *clustering* and *outlining*. They resulted in five-paragraph essays that reflect the outline model demonstrated in Chapter 10. Other essays are protracted paragraphs with clearly defined beginnings, middles, and ends.

Daily Lesson Plan

1. *Writing Lab (8–10 minutes)*

The Writing Lab consists of giving the students *three* separate topics from the list in Chapter 13. These topics and questions have proven to be sure-fire writing starters. The students should write for about eight to ten minutes to complete the three paragraphs.

Hint: Tell the students to place a check next to the paragraph they consider to be their best writing. Ask the students to use examples whenever possible.

2. *Spelling (5 minutes)*

On the back of the Writing Lab paper, quiz the students on ten words from the list of "Most Commonly Misspelled Words." The students should correct their own papers and keep an account of their spelling progress. Allow them approximately five minutes to complete the quiz.

Gerald E. Forrest

3. *Grammar (12 minutes)*

The teacher may choose any good grammar workbook and have the students do one or two exercises on any topic that has proven to be a trouble spot for the class. The students should be allowed approximately twelve minutes to complete this exercise.

4. *Lesson for the Day: Short Essays (with Recommended Exercises, 30 minutes)*

Many of the writings in this section are a result of one- or two-word topics given as homework assignments. The students were asked to cluster, outline, and write five-paragraphs on such topics as:

"Happiness"
"Peace"
"My Hero"
"Teddy Bears"
"TV Today"

Happiness

Happiness is skipping through a secret meadow as a spring breeze showers you with colorful blossoms.

Happiness is little children laughing and smiling, and friendly passersby saying, "Hello."

Happiness is self-confidence and the feeling that you're going to burst with uncontrollable laughter.

Happiness is optimism, cheerfulness, and hope.

Happiness is caring about somebody and feeling free to express yourself. It's knowing you have values, talents, and priorities such as honor, integrity, intelligence, success, and a joy for life.

Happiness is like a sparkling gem—all want to obtain it but few know how to go about it. You are your key to happiness.

—Krystle

Peace

Peace is running as fast and as hard as you can until you collapse into a plush patch of warm and sweet smelling grass, causing you to drift off to sleep.

Peace is twirling yourself around and around until you are too dizzy to walk.

Peace is watching the sun set and the moon rise, all the while noticing the way they reflect their light upon the surrounding wheat fields.

Peace is sitting on your bedroom windowsill reading a book on a rainy day, breathing in tune with the pitter-patter.

Peace is going to a private pond to feed the animals as you tell them of your troubled day.

Peace means different things to different people. Only you know how to achieve peace.

—*Krystle*

My Hero

Who is my hero?

Is a hero someone who can score sixty points in one basketball game; someone that wins four Grammy awards? Is a hero an athlete, an actor? Do heroes have to be tall, strong, rich? To some people, most definitely.

My hero stands tall at just under six feet. He is a casual man that couldn't be singled out in a crowd of twenty.

My hero was there to hug me when I first struck out in Little League. He was there to cheer when I hit a buzzer-beater in basketball. My hero taught me everything I know about life, on issues ranging from free throws to chess. My hero will urge me to get back up and "walk it off" when I feel pain.

Some call my hero "Mr. Aetan," some call him "Gilbert," and some even call him "Sir"; but I am fortunate enough to call him "Dad."

—*Adam*

Gerald E. Forrest

Teddy Bears

Teddy bears are one of people's best friends, yet they don't get much credit. I feel this is very wrong.

When you were young, you appreciated the value of a good teddy bear, such as its security and comfort in those critical and rocky young years. They fought off monsters and everything. You never slept without them.

As you got older, you tended to forget how compassionate a teddy bear can be. When you were down in the dumps, when you were cold and scared—how warm and cuddly they were!

I think most people know how cheerful and joyous teddy bears are, when you're on top of the world. Teddy bears bring back funny and sad memories alike. Never forget when you were upset, how one hug from your teddy bear made everything in the world feel right.

Teddy bears are an important part of growing up, but they never should be forgotten, because without an adorable teddy bear, the world would be an awfully cold place.

—Krystle

Television Violence

Television is a powerful influence in our lives, especially for young children. Research shows that an elementary school-age child watches an average of four hours of television each day. That works out to be 1,460 hours per year, or the equivalent of 61 days.

One should use television to entertain, educate, and inform. Viewing programs that help to inform our children of current events, news, and history is a good thing. It is when our young people are unsupervised while watching TV that problems arise.

Watching programs that contain endless violence is certainly harmful to children. Children remember much of what they see on television. They are likely to form ideas and attitudes about life and the world around them, thinking it's okay to be aggressive and violent.

Television viewing can hurt children when they are unable to distinguish between right and wrong. When violence is used to solve problems in television programming, this sends the wrong message. From television's provocation, many people become violent in society and find themselves in jail.

Therefore, less television violence would benefit our society. Violence should never be used to solve our daily problems. In the end, it is usually the innocent that fall victim to violence.

—Brendan

TV Today

TV today has many programs that show violent scenes. Some people consider this very educational because it shows how many parts of the body operate.

Some shows illustrate how much blood you have in your body. For example, when someone hits an artery of another person, blood squirts out everywhere.

Sometimes in a movie about knights, battle scenes will show someone's kidney or intestines being exposed from an ax or knife wound. If you go to see a horror movie, it will show someone's heart being pulled out of his or her chest. You get to see how the heart pumps and works.

The medical dramas on TV will show victims of violence and what happens to them and their bodies, which teaches you how a body functions.

This is why I think violence on TV is educational.

—Matt

5. *Recommended Exercises*

First, have the students choose a subject they feel strongly about. Then have them cluster their ideas, make an outline, and write a five-paragraph theme expressing their personal opinions and feelings about the subject. Finish and improve for homework what they have started in class.

12

Pictures as a Start for Writing

In this exercise the students are encouraged to let their imaginations go to work on a visual prop such as a picture. The students may describe what they see, or build a short story around the picture or object.

Action pictures seem to serve as good starts to stimulate the writing process, especially for younger writers, as shown in the examples that follow.

Daily Lesson Plan

1. *Writing Lab (8–10 minutes)*

The Writing Lab consists of giving the students *three* separate topics from the list in Chapter 13. These topics and questions have proven to be sure-fire writing starters. The students should write for about eight to ten minutes to complete the three paragraphs.

Hint: Tell the students to place a check next to the paragraph they consider to be their best writing. Ask the students to use examples whenever possible.

2. *Spelling (5 minutes)*

On the back of the Writing Lab paper, quiz the students on ten words from the list of "Most Commonly Misspelled Words." The students should correct their own papers and keep an account of their spelling progress. Allow them approximately five minutes to complete the quiz.

3. *Grammar (12 minutes)*

The teacher may choose any good grammar workbook and have the students do one or two exercises on any topic that has

proven to be a trouble spot for the class. The students should be allowed approximately twelve minutes to complete this exercise.

4. *Lesson for the Day: Pictures as a Start for Writing (with Recommended Exercises, 30 minutes)*

Collect pictures from books, calendars, post cards, and so forth, and have the students write something about them. The following are short examples inspired by looking at pictures:

[A picture from a magazine of a storm-damaged pier] *"On a dark misty morning I come upon a mythological-looking structure encased in the thick fog . . ."*

—*Jim*

[A photograph of a skydiver] *"With a hint of hesitation, I leaped from the security of the airplane and found myself almost unbelievably floating downward . . ."*

—*Michael*

[An illustration of an alien] *"It was a cold October night, and the wind was howling and blowing about the dancing leaves . . ."*

—*Jason*

[A picture of a student's room] *"You arrive upon a bedroom door. There are drawings and posters covering it, as if to be a collage . . ."*

—*Vincent*

[A picture of girls at lunch in the school cafeteria] *"It is Monday afternoon. My friends and I were in the cafeteria discussing the upcoming concert starring all of our favorite bands."*

—*Krystle*

[A magazine picture of a storm-damaged pier] *"On a dark misty morning, I come upon a mythological-looking structure encased in the fog. As I approach the large structure, I wonder its purpose on this desolate stretch of ocean shore. I* notice that it is some type of ancient building from the Greeks. When I step onto it, there seems to be sand underneath. I walk on it for a minute or two and feel the thick, wet, and grainy sand come up between my toes. I ask myself, 'Have I found the home of Zeus?'"

—Jim

[A photograph of a young girl] *"This is a picture of my sister. She is standing in front of a large bush. It looks like it is about ten in the morning, because of the way the sun is shining. She has brown hair that is long and soft looking. Her shirt is white and her face is pale. She is my sister and she looks like an angel."*

—Travis

The following five paragraph themes were also inspired by pictures:

[A picture of a teenage boy with three small children] *If I were to babysit three little urchins, then I would need to make a plan. To prepare this plan, I would ask the three children what things they would like to do. We would then make a calendar showing what we would be doing each day that I babysat. This would also help me know what to bring each time I went to their house.*

The first thing we would probably do is to play games like a popular board game. The other games they may like to play are Twister or checkers.

On another day, we would go to the park and bring a picnic lunch. At one park in the valley we would play frisbee golf. The kids like this, and it would use up a lot of time.

Next, we would sing songs and dance. Arts and crafts would be next. We would paint frogs and draw on the sidewalk with chalk. We would also read stories and even make plays about the stories we read.

The plan I've devised for babysitting will need to work because it's the only plan I have.

—Matt

[A magazine illustration of a skydiver] *With a hint of hesitation, I leaped from the security of the airplane and found myself almost unbelievably floating downward. The checkerboard design of the landscape lay before me while the deep blue sky loomed above.*

The roar of the airplane engine began to fade, replaced only by the intense hiss of the wind as it rushed by my ears. The force of air against my body was so strong that it seemed to be the only thing holding me up.

All the while I kept thinking I must be crazy. But the desire to jump from an airplane and freefall into nothingness is an even stronger emotion.

Only when I finally pulled the ripcord that instantly released the parachute from it's pack, did I once again feel secure enough to enjoy the rest of my trip downward.

—Michael

[A photograph of a girl's bedroom] *My room is very pretty. It is cozy and quaint. I guess you'd call it my room.*

It has two pictures that hang above the side of my bed. One picture is of a black man holding a baby, and the second is of an African woman carving a doll.

On the wall across from my bed is what I call my "cute wall." It has my baseball and zoo pennants, birthday balloons, a porcelain ballet slipper, and my stereo.

On the other side of my bed is my cute Victorian-style dresser with a window over it. On the wall which has the door is my desk.

All in all, I really love my room and would never change anything.

—Krystle

[A picture of an overgrown yard] *Well, this is the day I've been dreading. I have to cut the weeds in the backyard. The weeds have been growing all winter until now. They are huge masses of green stalks gleaming with morning dew. The stalks are over my head, creating a virtual jungle that I have to face.*

First, I have to gather some equipment for my mission. I look out at the spider-filled garage and ask myself if I really want to search through the many dangerous traps for a Weed Whacker. I think not. With this decision I pull together some weed-chopping tools. First, I get a machete, then a stick with a knife on the end, and last, I attach a knife blade to a boot.

As I walk out to the backyard, crisp air rushes over my face, bringing the smell of vegetation with it. As I walk towards the jungle, I notice the ground is damp, but despite this I take out the gleaming blade. I send the blade flying, and it slices through the growth with slashing sounds.

After a long time of chopping, I finally come to the end of the yard. The sun is starting to go down, giving the sky a purple hue.

I am tired and exhausted when I finally finish; the weeds cover the ground like a green blanket. I walk inside. I'm glad that my job is over. Suddenly I think, "I will have to mow the lawn weekly from now until the end of summer.

—*David*

[A newspaper ad for a rodeo coming to town] *"What the heck am I doing on a bull?" I thought to myself. The last thing I remember was sitting at my desk at home writing a paper for my Language Arts class when everything went black. When I woke up, I was sitting on a raging bull.*

The bull is rocking back and forth, snorting hot air from his nostrils, getting ready for the battle to come. We are both pinned inside a rusty cage, the bull kicking up puffs of foul smelling dust. I am scared out of my mind. One, I am on a raging bull, and, two, I'm in some terrible rodeo clothes. The worst possible thing happens—the cage opens.

The bull bolts out, and I am flung in the air like a rag doll, barely hanging on by the horn of the beaten saddle. I land on my side, and pain shoots up my back. My muscles tighten up at the pain of the bull's bucking. This sends my hands convulsing, making it harder to hold on.

The bull bucks left, and I am pushed right. I hold on but my finger slips, sending me flying through the air. I hit the ground with a crackling thump. The bull charges forward at me. I try to get up, but I realize that my leg is snapped. The bull rears up, its giant hooves in my face. Then they come down, and everything becomes black.

I wake up in a hospital bed, covered with bandages and casts. I can't move or talk, but I say to myself, "Self, you're never going to write about a bull again."

—Jason

[A picture of racing canoes on a river] *The hot afternoon sun baked down upon my sweat-covered back. I looked out across the wide rushing river and slowly panned towards the rapids that splashed white water over the jagged rocks, protruding from places unseen. This was a good day for a race.*

A numb feeling ran down my legs as I stretched, a normal pre-race routine. Swinging my arms provided me with an adrenaline rush and prepared them for the strenuous rowing that would take place in the next five minutes. My rowing team consisted of five men including myself. This would be our seventh national race. Out of those seven, we finished first once and were in the top five of the others.

The speaker clicked on, and the starter announced the start of the countdown. I quickly grabbed my oar and stuck it in ready position. We took off with a bang of the starting gun. I paddled faster and faster. The water sprayed in my face felt good. As we darted with the current, the sweat ran down my face as I stroked. My arms began to tire. A tight feeling hung in my stomach.

"We're almost there." John, the team captain, yelled. We had pulled in front. Now my arms were painfully numbed. I could barely lift the oar out of the water to paddle.

"Stop!" John yelled as we flew past the finish line. I didn't know if we had won, as a yellow canoe floated past us. No, we had not won this one, but there will always be next time.

—Eric

[A magazine picture of a storm-damaged pier] *I was heartbroken when I discovered my Roman ruin was only the weather-beaten, splintered pilings of an old dilapidated pier. It is amazing the difference that distance makes on my perception. In particular it seems to alter the function, structural material, and size of an object.*

I did not see the Roman Forum where the subjects were ruled. It was just a place where old men and little boys stopped to fish with long sticks and a knotted piece of string tied to a hook.

The ancient marble columns I saw from the beach became peeling, damp, wooden posts when I neared them.

What I thought was a marble hall the size of a gymnasium was really just an old fishing pier the size of a racquetball court.

Perspective is deceiving. It changes the appearance of what we see. It appears to change the size, use, and substance. It turned a dilapidated fishing pier into an ancient Roman ruin. Perspective can determine how we see things.

—Eric

[A picture of a fire-eater performance] *As I watched the crowd grow, I grew curious. I walked towards them. They were all in some kind of mass hysteria.*

I made my way farther and farther towards the middle of the crowd. I was amazed at the enthusiastic "oohs!" and "aahs!" I heard coming from the mouths of people all around me. As I came closer towards the center of the hype, I could see fire torches flying through the air somewhat to a rhythmic motion. First one, then two, and then three. Yes, there were three wooden sticks engulfed with flames rising up and above the crowd. By the time I made it to the center of the circle, the act was over.

Next, I saw the brown Muslim man take a torch and put it in his mouth. The expression on his face was ghastly and terrifying as if something had gone wrong. Much to my amazement, he removed the torch uninjured and blew. It wasn't like he blew out air, he was blowing fire.

All of a sudden, the clapping and yelling of the crowd engulfed me. I saw money flying over my head. The man seemed appreciative and then left.

As the crowd dissipated, I recalled the event I had just witnessed. Amazing! That was the only word that I could think of to describe this astounding act.

—Eric

5. *Recommended Exercises*

Choose a picture from a magazine and build a story around it.

13

Questions and Statements

Few people say they like to write unless they are good writers. Most of us have a natural aversion to writing because it demands thinking, planning, and effort.

That is why this chapter is so necessary and effective. It is a chapter that encourages the writer to write about the most important thing in the world, himself. This chapter capitalizes on that part of human nature which has a need to share and tell his or her story. These questions and statements will help students focus on topics that they know and have opinions about, and hence serve as a springboard to creativity.

Without these questions and student responses, this book would not have been possible.

Questions and Statements

1. What does a high school diploma mean to me?

2. How important is it to have a good friend?

3. What makes for a good friendship?

4. My favorite charity is . . . because . . .

5. If I were to win the lottery, I would . . .

6. A dream vacation for me would be to . . .

7. My happiest birthday was . . .

8. When I have children I will teach them to . . .

9. Why is it so hard for people to get along?

10. How do I feel when people reject me?

11. A day I'd like to forget was . . .

12. What is uppermost on my mind today?

13. It's tough being a teenager these days, because . . .

14. Why are good manners important?

15. My favorite room in the house is . . .

16. What do I like about America?

17. I can't wait until . . .

18. Getting along with my brother/sister is difficult because . . .

19. I'm not very good at . . .

20. The thing I do best is . . .

21. I wish I could . . .

22. What part of my life is going the way I want it to?

23. What will I do this weekend?

24. The advice I would give to teachers is . . .

25. What do I look for in a car?

26. How do I feel when someone I love cries?

27. Was there a time a person wouldn't listen to me?

28. On a scale of 1–10, how is my day going?

29. I like animals, especially . . .

30. What have I discovered about myself this past week?

31. A person I feel safe with is . . .

32. A time I said something I didn't mean was . . .

33. The best compliment I have ever received was . . .

34. My worst experience was . . .

35. My finest hour was when . . .

36. The boy/girl I marry will be great, because . . .

37. I like certain kinds of people, such as . . .

38. The nickname I like best is . . . because . . .

39. The best day I can remember is . . .

40. Describe yourself five years from now.

41. If I had one month to live, I would . . .

42. What does perfume remind me of?

43. What is the highlight of my life?

44. What do I wish were different in my life?

45. My best friend is . . .

46. Describe your physical body.

47. Am I a giver or a taker?

48. What do I most fear?

49. What's missing in my life?

50. What kind of people make me tense?

51. Three good qualities I have are . . .

52. A place I'd like to visit is . . .

53. What is my chief flaw?

54. What do my friends say about me?

55. Everybody has a turning point in his or her life. Mine was . . .

56. Three things that I would like to accomplish during my lifetime are . . .

57. What I like about school is . . .

58. My favorite grammar school teacher was . . .

59. My new job is challenging because . . .

60. What do I think of cigarette smoking?

61. What was the biggest surprise in my life?

62. My favorite story is . . . because . . .

63. Describe someone you would want to be like.

64. If I could spend tomorrow with anyone in the world, it would be . . .

65. The thing I resent most about adults is . . .

66. There will (or will not) be a war in my lifetime, because . . .

67. My pet peeve is . . .

68. The best Christmas gift I have ever given someone was . . .

69. The politician I admire most is . . .

70. The one place in my life I would like to return to is . . .

71. Three goals I would like to accomplish this month are . . .

72. Write out a plan to accomplish life's goals.

73. My plans for the summer are . . .

74. Given three wishes, what would they be?

75. Another time period in which I would like to have lived was . . .

76. If I were a parent . . .

77. Sometimes I am really concerned about . . .

78. Should our country get involved in foreign wars? Explain.

79. If I had my own TV show, it would be . . .

80. My dream car is . . .

81. I wish the government would spend more money on . . .

82. Do you want to go to college?

83. How important is work to you?

84. How to approach the serious responsibility of driving a car . . .

85. Describe a perfect school day.

86. What has been my biggest regret?

87. What was my "Road Not Taken?"

88. What is my fondest memory?

89. Who has been the biggest influence in my life?

90. What was my proudest moment?

91. Was there a person whose very presence thrilled me?

92. Was there a time I scorned someone?

93. What was the most precious thing I have given to another?

94. What am I most grateful for?

95. Is there a person I have a difficult time forgiving?

96. When was the loneliest time of my life?

97. What was a valuable lesson I have learned?

98. Am I a good manager of my moods?

About the Author

Gerald Forrest received his Bachelor of Arts in English from St. Mary's College of California in 1956. In 1964, Mr. Forrest earned a master's degree from Loyola University of Los Angeles in Counseling and Guidance.

A licensed Marriage, Family, and Child Counselor in the state of California, Mr. Forrest holds a Pupil Personnel Certificate as well as a Life Credential in Secondary Education. Mr. Forrest has been teaching and counseling in private and public schools for the past forty-seven years.

The techniques and writing exercises put forth in this book by Mr. Forrest result from the last twelve years of teaching Language Arts during summer school.